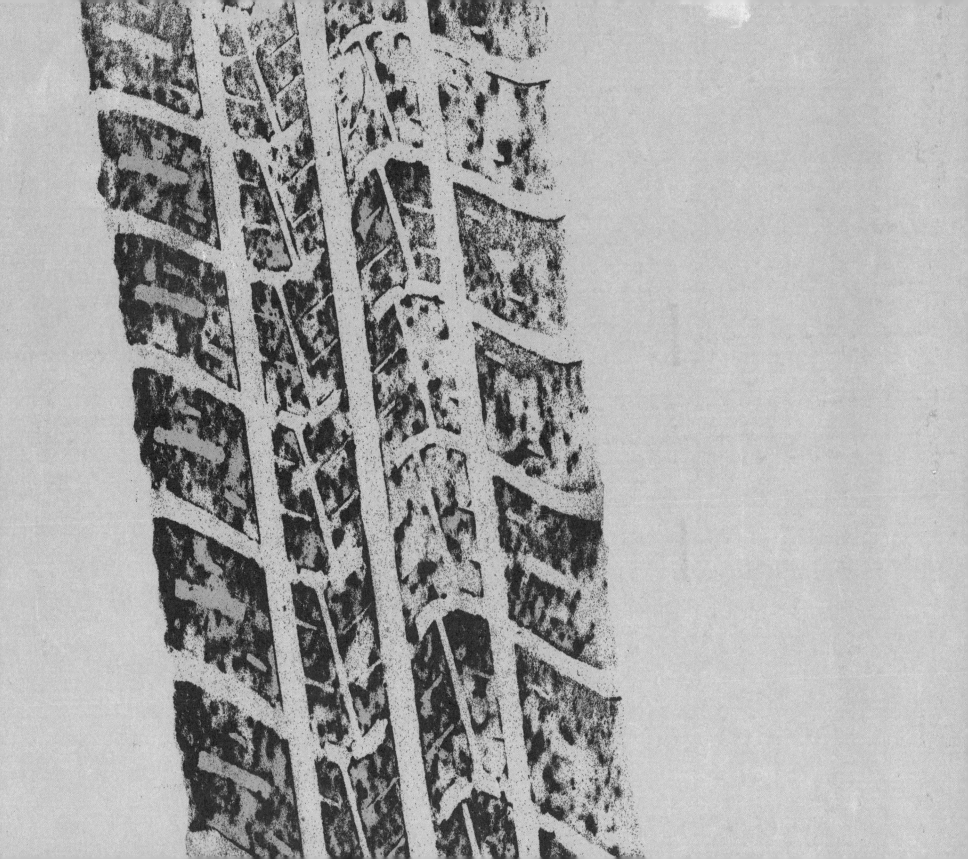

I DRIVE A
FREIGHT TRAIN

by **Sarah Bridges**

illustrated by **Amy Bailey Muehlenhardt**

PICTURE WINDOW BOOKS
Minneapolis, Minnesota

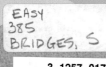

Thank you to Robert Hawkins for the train wisdom and great stories. S.B.

Editor: Jill Kalz

Designer: Jaime Martens

Page Production: Tracy Kaehler

Creative Director: Keith Griffin

Editorial Director: Carol Jones

The illustrations in this book were created digitally.

Printed in the United States of America.

Picture Window Books

5115 Excelsior Boulevard

Suite 232

Minneapolis, MN 55416

877-845-8392

www.picturewindowbooks.com

Library of Congress Cataloging-in-Publication Data

Bridges, Sarah.

I drive a freight train / by Sarah Bridges ; illustrated by Amy Bailey Muehlenhardt.

p. cm. — (Working wheels)

Includes bibliographical references and index.

ISBN 1-4048-1607-0 (hardcover)

1. Railroads—Juvenile literature. 2. Locomotive engineers—Juvenile literature. I. Muehlenhardt, Amy Bailey, 1974– . II. Title. III. Series: Bridges, Sarah. Working wheels.

TF148.B72 2005

385'.36'092—dc22   2005023143

Thanks to our advisers for their expertise, research, and advice:

Jim Wrinn, Editor
Trains Magazine, Waukesha, Wisconsin

Susan Kesselring, M.A., Literacy Educator
Rosemount—Apple Valley—Eagan (Minnesota) School District

My name is Marcia, and I'm an engineer.
I drive a freight train.

Trains run on tracks. Tracks are made of metal rails and support pieces that lie on a bed of rock.

Before each trip, conductors walk around their trains to make sure everything is in good condition. They also make sure the cars are loaded with the correct freight.

There are two seats inside. One seat is for me, and the other is for my conductor, Lou. The conductor is in charge of the whole train.

First, I move the throttle, and the locomotive slowly backs up. It hooks up with the other cars. I move the throttle again, and the train pulls forward.

Unlike the rubber wheels on a car or truck, train wheels are made of metal. A wide piece of metal on the side of each wheel helps the train stay on the track.

I push a lever to test the freight train's brakes. WHOOSH! It sounds like air being let out of a balloon. This sound means the brakes are working. Then I test the horn.

Engineers sound the horn to let people know that a train is nearing a street crossing.

My freight train carries many different
kinds of things. I haul coal, cars and trucks,
oil, or food. Today, many of the train cars
are filled with lightbulbs.

Meat, lettuce, ice cream, and other freight that must be kept cold are hauled in refrigerated cars. Bulky objects are hauled on cars with no sides or tops. These cars are called flatcars.

Colored lights on the sides of the tracks tell me when I can go. These lights are called wayside signals. They flash like stoplights.

Engineers control a train's speed with hand levers instead of a gas pedal.

In the United States, freight trains average about 25 miles (40 kilometers) per hour.

We chug along through the countryside.
I see fields, rivers, and farmhouses. I even
roll through mountains!

A freight train usually pulls about 100 cars and weighs thousands of tons. Trying to stop it is like trying to stop a running elephant! I can't stop quickly. I have to start slowing down long before I reach a station.

In an emergency, a conductor or engineer can use the train's emergency brake. But even with this brake, a freight train still needs more than 1 mile (1.6 kilometers) to stop.

19

Freight train engineers may go on long or short trips. On long trips, they sleep in hotels along the way. They leave their trains parked on an extra track at the station. For very long trips, more than one crew may drive the train.

Once my train has stopped, a crew checks the engine. They refill any fluids that are low. If this is the last stop on my trip, all of the freight is unloaded. Otherwise, I lock the train for the night and start again in the morning.

FREIGHT TRAIN DIAGRAM

cab

locomotive

cars

tracks

GLOSSARY

cab—the place where the driver, or engineer, of a train sits

car—a vehicle that moves on railroad tracks

conductor—a person who is in charge on a train

engineer—a person who drives a train

fluids—liquids in the engine that make it run smoothly

freight—goods that are shipped from one place to another

locomotive—the engine car

throttle—a lever that makes a train move forward or backward

FUN FACTS

 When freight trains move in or out of stations, they travel at 4 miles (6.4 kilometers) per hour or less. That is about the same speed as a fast walk.

 Freight trains have fuel tanks that hold between 2,300 and 2,500 gallons (8,740 and 9,500 liters) of fuel. Most automobiles hold about 15 gallons (57 liters) of fuel.

 In the United States, freight trains move 15 billion tons (13.5 billion metric tons) of freight each year. The total worth of that freight is about $9 trillion!

 Freight trains travel rain or shine. When heavy snow falls, a special train travels down the tracks first. It clears them like a snowplow.

TO LEARN MORE

At the Library

Rex, Michael. *My Freight Train*. New York: Henry Holt, 2002.

Richardson, Adele. *Freight Trains*. Mankato, Minn.: Capstone Press, 2001.

Stille, Darlene. *Freight Trains*. Minneapolis: Compass Point Books, 2001.

On the Web

FactHound offers a safe, fun way to find Internet sites related to this book. All of the sites on FactHound have been researched by our staff.

1. Visit www.facthound.com

2. Type in this special code for age-appropriate sites: 1404816070

3. Click on the FETCH IT button.

Your trusty FactHound will fetch the best sites for you!

INDEX

LOOK FOR ALL OF THE BOOKS IN THE WORKING WHEELS SERIES:

- I Drive a Backhoe
  1-4048-1604-6
- I Drive a Bulldozer
  1-4048-0613-X
- I Drive a Crane
  1-4048-1605-4
- I Drive a Dump Truck
  1-4048-0614-8

- I Drive a Fire Engine
  1-4048-1606-2
- I Drive a Freight Train
  1-4048-1607-0
- I Drive a Garbage Truck
  1-4048-0615-6
- I Drive an Ambulance
  1-4048-0618-0

- I Drive a Semitruck
  1-4048-0616-4
- I Drive a Snowplow
  1-4048-0617-2
- I Drive a Street Sweeper
  1-4048-1608-9
- I Drive a Tractor
  1-4048-1609-7

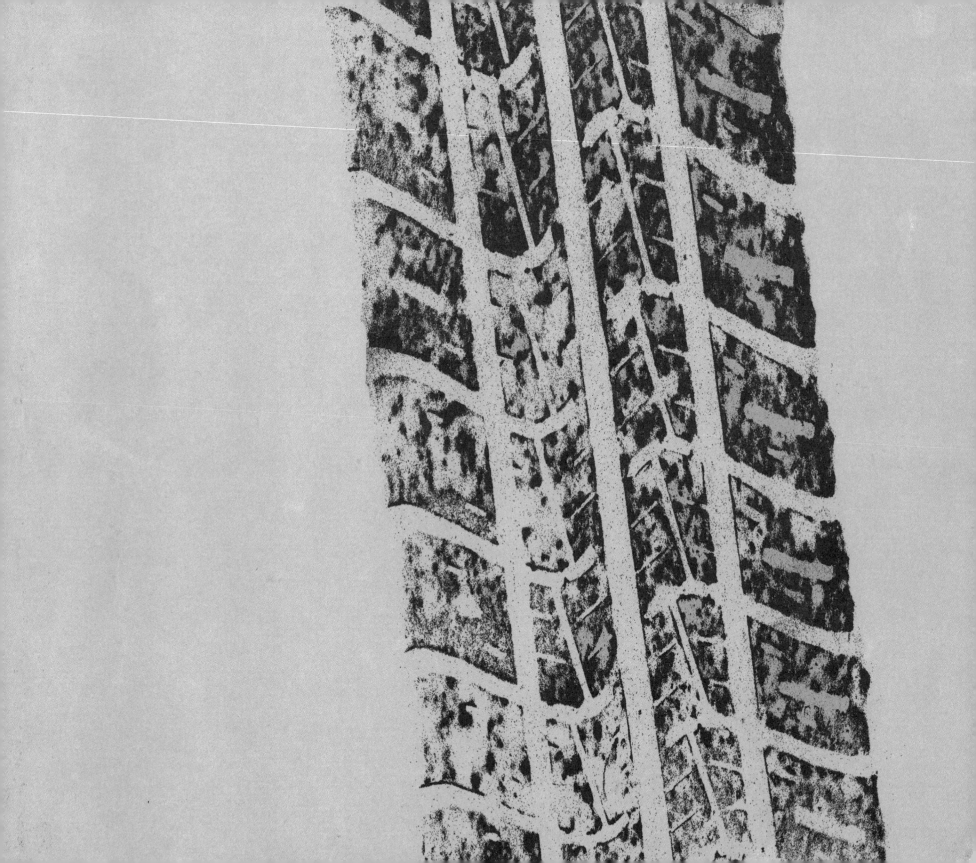